# RUSSIAN GIRL

## Life in an
## Old Russian Town

### RUSS KENDALL

SCHOLASTIC
HARDCOVER

SCHOLASTIC INC. • New York

This is Olga Surikova. She is nine. Her family name is Surikov. But, like all Russian girls and women, her last name ends with the letter "a."

The Surikov family lives in a two-bedroom apartment. Most families in town live in one-bedroom apartments. Because Olga's parents work so hard, they can afford a bigger home. They even own a little television. Many families do not.

Olga's father, Vladimir, is a carpenter. To make extra money, he paints and repairs cars. Elena, her mother, is a nurse. She also works part-time in a tourist hotel. Olga's brother, Ivan, is ten. And Cheena is the dog.

3

The Surikovs live in a small Russian town called Suzdal. It's 150 miles east of Moscow, the capital city of Russia. Suzdal is nearly 1,000 years old. About 10,000 people live there — old Russian war heroes, dancers, policemen, teachers, workers, farmers, and many others. The weather in Suzdal is similar to that in northern New England. It is warm and sunny in the summer and then cold and snowy in the winter. The Surikov family has lived in Suzdal for many generations.

The Kamenka River runs right through the middle of Suzdal. When the weather is nice, art students sit on the riverbank and sketch the town. Old women do their laundry at the river's edge. Elena does almost all of her laundry at home, by hand in the bathtub.

6

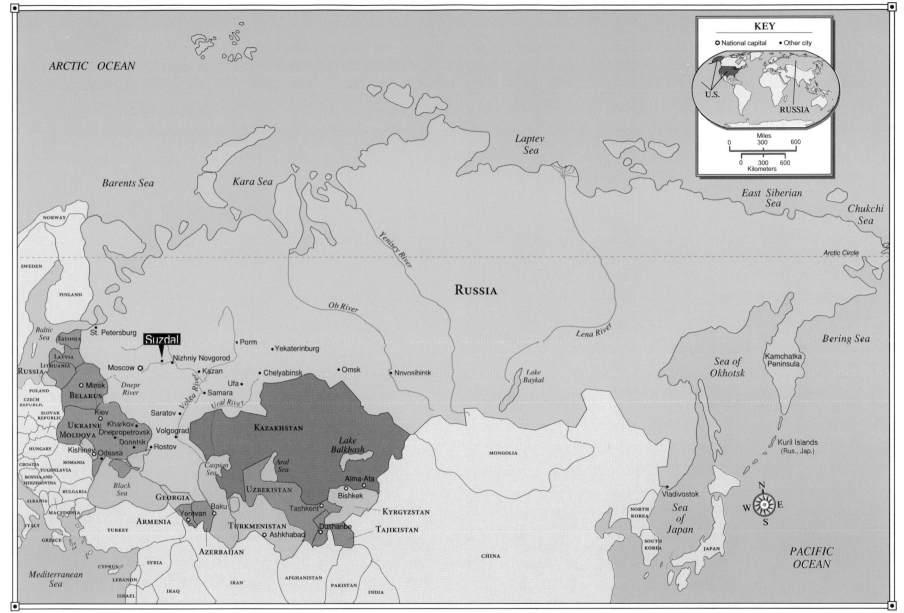

Laptev
Sea

ARCTIC OCEAN

Barents Sea

Kara Sea

East Siberian
Sea

Chukchi
Sea

Arctic Circle

NORWAY

SWEDEN

FINLAND

RUSSIA

Bering
Sea

Kamchatka
Peninsula

Baltic
Sea

St. Petersburg

Suzdal

Porm

Yekaterinburg

Moscow

Nizhniy Novgorod

Kazan

Omsk

Novosibirsk

Lake
Baykal

Sea of
Okhotsk

ESTONIA

LATVIA

LITHUANIA

Minsk

Dnepr
River

Ufa

Chelyabinsk

Volga River

BELARUS

POLAND

Samara

Kuril Islands
(Rus., Jap.)

CZECH
REPUBLIC

SLOVAK
REPUBLIC

Kiev

Kharkov

Saratov

Ural River

MONGOLIA

UKRAINE

MOLDOVA

Dnepropetrovsk

Volgograd

KAZAKHSTAN

HUNGARY

Donetsk

Rostov

Lake
Balkhash

Vladivostok

Kishinev

Odessa

CROATIA

ROMANIA

Caspian
Sea

Aral
Sea

NORTH
KOREA

Sea
of
Japan

BOSNIA AND
HERZEGOVINA

YUGOSLAVIA

BULGARIA

Black
Sea

GEORGIA

Alma-Ata

ALBANIA

MACEDONIA

ARMENIA

Yerevan

Baku

UZBEKISTAN

Bishkek

KYRGYZSTAN

SOUTH
KOREA

JAPAN

ITALY

TURKEY

TURKMENISTAN

Tashkent

Dushanbe

TAJIKISTAN

CHINA

PACIFIC
OCEAN

GREECE

CYPRUS

SYRIA

Ashkhabad

AZERBAIJAN

Mediterranean
Sea

LEBANON

ISRAEL

IRAQ

IRAN

AFGHANISTAN

PAKISTAN

INDIA

Yenisey River

Ob River

Lena River

RUSSIA

RUSSIA

All countries shown in color on the large map were once part of the Soviet Union.

Russia is the biggest country in the world. It is almost twice as big as the United States. If you cross all of Russia, you will travel through eleven time zones. If you cross the United States from New York to California, you will travel through only four time zones.

In early September, Olga begins third grade. Her teacher, Lidiya Mihaylovna Pankratova, frightens Olga a little because she looks so stern. Olga likes reading and writing, but she finds math difficult. She hopes that Lidiya Mihaylovna won't call on her. Twice a week, the class will study English. Olga is excited about this, as she has seen pictures of the United States in books and on television, and she hopes to go there someday.

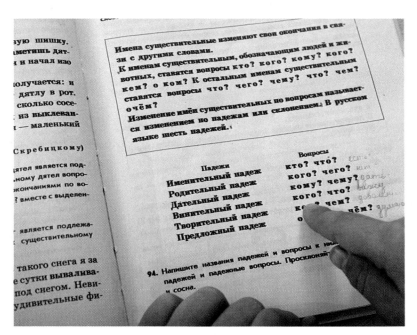

People in Russia use the Cyrillic alphabet. It's very different from the alphabet used in English, though a few of the letters are similar. Some Cyrillic letters are from the Greek alphabet.

At mid-morning, Olga's teacher lets the class take a short break in the hallway. Olga makes friends with Nina and Ulla, two new students. They are a little nervous, too. Nina tells them how last night her mother caught a fox in their garden and hit it with a stick until it fell down dead. But this morning, when Nina went to see it, it was gone. Ulla says that the fox was just pretending to be dead. Just then, Lidiya Mihaylovna calls everyone back into the classroom.

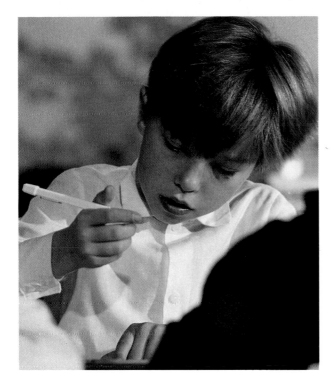

After the class returns to their seats, Lidiya Mihaylovna asks Olga to solve a math problem on the board in front of the class. Olga is scared, but she gets it right.

After school, Olga and Ivan visit their
*babushka*. That is the Russian word for
grandmother. Babushka has a small farm
nearby.

As they walk through the fields to milk the cows, Olga tells Babushka about the fox. Babushka says that foxes are very clever. Then she tells the children an old Russian folktale about a sly fox.

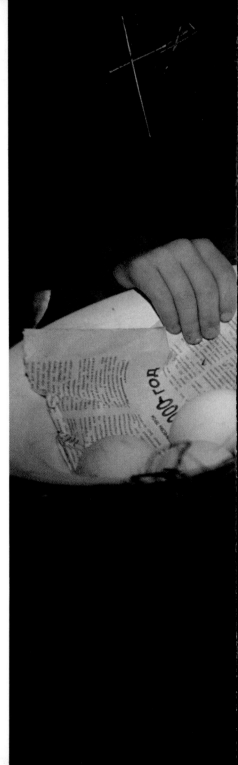

After milking the cows, Olga and Ivan help Babushka pour the milk through a cloth to catch any pieces of grass that might have fallen into the milking bucket. From her garden they get cabbages and potatoes and fresh parsley. From her chickens they get white eggs.

But Olga's favorites are the sweet green apples that come from the trees next to Babushka's garden. The trees make so many apples that Babushka is beginning to fill up a room in her house with them. The family will preserve these fruits and vegetables in jars and eat them all winter.

That night, after Olga finishes her homework, Vladimir asks her about her first day at school. Olga tells him about Lidiya Mihaylovna and making new friends and how difficult math is and about how much she wants to go to America.

Vladimir tells her that if she works hard and gets very high marks, someday he will take her there. He tells her she should spend at least an hour every night doing homework.

In the mornings, Vladimir walks to work. He makes tables and chairs in a woodshop not very far from the apartment. Sometimes after school Ivan visits the woodshop so he can learn about carpentry. On this day, his father shows him how to use the wood lathe. Ivan doesn't like all the sawdust that blows in his face.

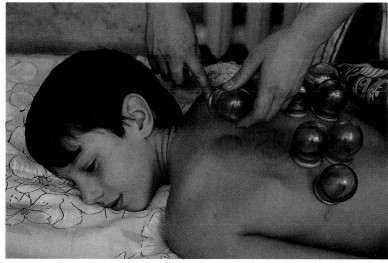

Although Elena is a nurse, she doesn't work in the town hospital. Instead, she works at home. When children don't feel well or are coughing a lot, parents can bring them to the Surikovs' apartment. Sometimes she "cups" them. This is an old Russian folk remedy. After she makes them lie down, she puts small, heated glass cups on the bare skin of their backs. As the glass cups cool down, the suction pulls a little bit of their skin inside the cup. Elena says that this draws away some of the bad blood. It doesn't hurt. After ten minutes, she takes the cups off. When she does this, each cup makes a popping sound. The cups leave red circles that go away after two weeks.

Olga and her family don't go to church very often. Few of the young families do, although many of them get baptized. Most of the older women in Suzdal go to church several times each day. They light candles and pray for their loved ones. There are thirty-three churches in Suzdal. All of them are Russian Orthodox.

When Elena needs something she can't get from Babushka's garden, she goes to the village market. Olga likes to go with her. Because of recent shortages, people never know when the market will run out of food. Some days there is almost nothing on the shelves at the store. In the big cities where there are no gardens, things are much harder.

In Russia, people buy things with rubles. A ruble is divided into 100 kopeks, the same way a dollar is divided into 100 cents.

By October, Olga has spent an hour every night studying her lessons, as her father instructed. But Vladimir feels that Olga's marks are not high enough. She must now study two hours each night until her grades improve. This makes Olga cry because she doesn't want her father to be disappointed in her. As her mother picks her up, Olga promises to work harder.

On the way to school the next morning, Olga notices how much colder it is. The leaves are changing color, and the wind is blowing right through her coat. She looks forward to winter and playing in the snow. Then she remembers what she promised her father and hurries on to school.

Each day at school, one student must serve
lunch to the rest of the class. Today it's Olga's
turn. First, she cleans and sets the table.
When her classmates arrive, she brings each
of them a small bowl of fish soup, a pancake
with some sour cream, a grated carrot salad,
and a small piece of hearty, dark bread.

While eating her bread, Olga discovers that one of her baby teeth is loose. Her loose tooth makes it hard to pay attention to her lessons.

After school, Olga visits her friend, Yuri Yuryevich Yuryev. He rings the bells at the monastery once every hour to let all the people in town know what time it is. Yuri lets Olga help. When it becomes too loud, Olga covers her ears.

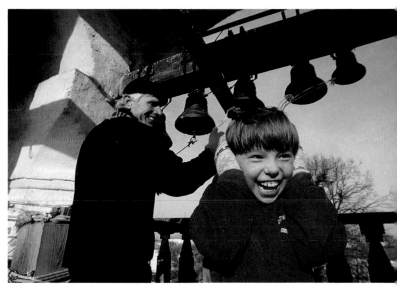

When Yuri Yuryevich was a baby, his parents were killed in World War II. He had nearly starved to death before someone brought him to a monastery in Suzdal. The nurses who took care of him named him. The monks raised him, and when he finished school, he returned to the monastery to work and ring the bells.

Later, Olga spends two hours doing homework.
Then she plays outside with Cheena and Ivan until
it gets dark. They like to walk along the tops of
narrow walls and try to push each other off.

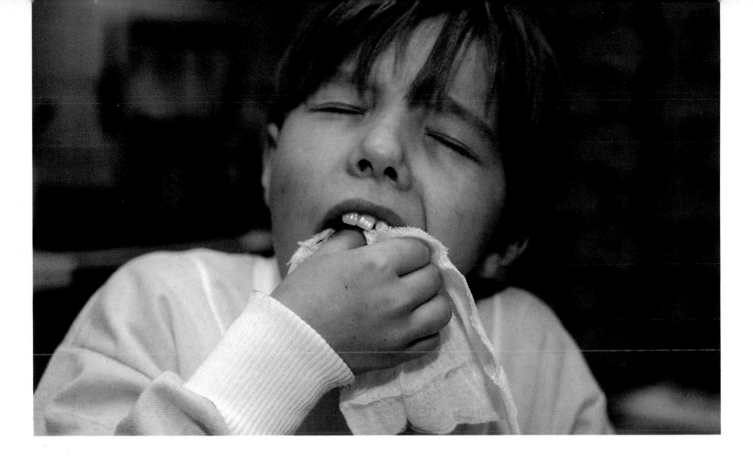

After dinner, Olga's tooth is very loose, and she pulls it out. When she shows her mother, Elena reminds her about the tooth mouse. "Throw your tooth under your bed before you go to sleep," she tells Olga.

That night, before she sleeps, Olga throws her tooth under the bed and says, "Mouse, Mouse, please take this tooth and bring me a new one." When Olga wakes up the next morning, the tooth under her bed is gone!

By early November, the first quarter of school is finished, and school vacation begins. It is very cold, and snow covers the ground. Some of the old men stand on the frozen Kamenka River and try to catch fish through the holes they cut in the ice.

Olga spends her first day of vacation playing in the snow with Ivan and Cheena and children from the other apartments. They build snow women out of rolled-up snowballs and then paint makeup on the snow women's faces. Even though she gets wet and a little cold, Olga stays outside until her mother calls her to come and help make dinner.

Tonight Olga and Elena are making a special dinner for Vladimir. He is celebrating his birthday. In Russia, people celebrate their birthdays twice — once for the day they were born and again for the day of the saint they are named for. The feastday of St. Vladimir is in July.

As Olga chops apples, Vladimir tells her how proud he is of her. She has studied hard, as she promised, and her grades are much improved.

Olga is no longer scared of her teacher, Lidiya Mihaylovna. But for the next two weeks of vacation, she will be very glad not to think about school.

# TWO RUSSIAN RECIPES

Two of Olga's favorite things to eat are beet and cabbage soup (*borsch*) and Russian apple pie (*pirog*). Every family has its own favorite recipe — some are very different. These are the recipes that Elena uses to make them. You and your parents or teachers can make the very same dinner that Olga and Elena make!

## *Pirog*

*INGREDIENTS:*

4 small apples
3 eggs
1 cup white sugar
1 cup flour
Dab of butter

*DIRECTIONS:*

1. Preheat the oven to 375 degrees Fahrenheit.
2. Cut cored, unpeeled apples into small pieces.
3. Mix eggs, sugar, and flour in a large bowl.
4. Rub a thin layer of butter inside a round 8-inch cake pan.
5. Place the chopped apples into the buttered pan.
6. Pour the egg mixture over the apples.
7. Bake for 35–40 minutes or until the top is golden brown.

When it's cool and firm, cut into slices. It's especially good with cold milk!

## *Borsch*

*INGREDIENTS:*

| | |
|---|---|
| 3 quarts water | 1 tomato |
| 1 teaspoon salt | ¼ cabbage |
| 1 pound of boneless pork* | 3 small potatoes |
| 1 big carrot | 2 cloves garlic |
| 1 large beet | Sour cream |
| 1 large white onion | Several sprigs parsley |
| 3 tablespoons oil | |

*Borsch is very good meatless or with beef or chicken.

*DIRECTIONS:*

1. Bring 3 quarts of water to a boil in a large stock pot.
2. Add 1 teaspoon of salt.
3. Cut pork into 1-inch cubes and add to the boiling water.
4. While the pork simmers, grate carrot and beet into a bowl.
5. Slice the onion and add to the bowl with the carrot and beet.
6. Heat 3 tablespoons of oil in a small skillet.
7. Mix the beet, onion, and carrot in the hot skillet for 5 minutes.
8. Add everything to the boiling water.
9. Chop up the tomato and add it to the water.
10. Slice the cabbage thinly and add it to the water.
11. Chop the potatoes and add them to the water.
12. Cover the pot, reduce the heat, and cook for 1 hour.

When it's ready to eat, ladle into a soup bowl, then add a little freshly minced garlic, a spoonful of sour cream, and a sprinkle of freshly chopped parsley on top. Eat while hot and steaming!

# ALPHABET

## Russian Cyrillic Alphabet with English Phonetic Sound Equivalents

There are no exact English equivalents to the 33 letters in the Cyrillic alphabet. Here is a very simplified guide that will help you understand many of the sounds made by Cyrillic letters. The hard sign and the soft sign have no sounds, but affect the sounds of the letters that come before them.

| Russian Cyrillic Capitals / Lowercase | Name of Cyrillic Letter | Pronunciation of Letter | Russian Cyrillic Capitals / Lowercase | Name of Cyrillic Letter | Pronunciation of Letter |
|---|---|---|---|---|---|
| А а | AH | (as in **fa**ther) | Р р | ERH* | (as in **r**ock) *the "**R**" is always rolled |
| Б б | BEH | (as in **b**elt) | С с | ES | (as in **s**ong) |
| В в | VEH | (as in **v**est) | Т т | TEH | (as in **t**epid) |
| Г г | GEH | (as in **g**et) | У у | OO | (as in b**oo**) |
| Д д | DEH | (as in **d**ent) | Ф ф | EF | (as in **f**all) |
| Е е | YEH | (as in **ye**t) | Х х | CHA | (as in the Scottish lo**ch**) |
| Ё ё | YO | (as in **yaw**n) | Ц ц | TSEH | (as in prin**ts**) |
| Ж ж | ZHE | (as in mea**s**ure) | Ч ч | CHEH | (as in **ch**unk) |
| З з | ZEH | (as in **z**eppelin) | Ш ш | SHA | (as in **sh**op) |
| И и | EE | (as in s**ee**k) | Щ щ | SHCHA | (fre**sh ch**eese) |
| Й й | YEE | (as in **yie**ld) | Ъ ъ | T'VYOR•day ZNAHK | (hard sign, no English equivalent) |
| К к | KAH | (as in **k**arate) | Ы ы | I | (as in h**i**ll) |
| Л л | EL | (as in **l**ove) | Ь ь | myach•KYAY ZNAHK | (soft sign, no English equivalent) |
| М м | EM | (as in **m**ight) | Э э | EH | (as in **e**nd) |
| Н н | EN | (as in **n**ight) | Ю ю | YEW | (as in **you**) |
| О о | AW | (as in d**o**g) | Я я | YAH | (as in **ya**cht) |
| П п | PEH | (as in **p**et) | | | |

## RUSSIAN WORDS

| English | Russian Pronunciation Guide | Russian |
|---|---|---|
| Grandmother | Babushka (BAH•bush•kah) | Бабушка |
| Grandfather | Dedushka (DYEH•doosh•kah) | Дедушка |
| Mother | Mama (MAH•mah) | Мама |
| Father | Papa (PAH•pah) | Папа |
| Brother | Brat (BRAHT) | Брат |
| Sister | Sestra (syeh•STRAH) | Сестра |
| Dog | Sobaka (sah•BAH•kah) | Собака |
| Cat | Kot (KAWT) | Кот |
| Milk | Moloko (mah•lah•KAW) | Молоко |
| Butter | Maslo (MAH•slah) | Масло |
| Apple | Yabloko (YAH•blah•kah) | Яблоко |
| Pie | Pirog (pee•RAWK) | Пирог |
| Sugar | Sakhar (SAH•khar) | Сахар |
| House | Dom (DAWM) | Дом |
| Town | Gorod (GAW•raht) | Город |
| Book | Kniga (K'NEE•gah) | Книга |
| Word | Slovo (SLAW•vah) | Слово |
| Letter (alphabet) | Bukva (BOOK•vah) | Буква |
| Snow | Sneg (SNYEK) | Снег |
| Tooth | Zub (ZOOP) | Зуб |
| School | Shkola (SHKAW•lah) | Школа |
| Zero | Nol (NAWLL) | Ноль |
| One | Odin (ah•DEEN) | Один |
| Two | Dva (DVAH) | Два |
| Three | Tri (TREE) | Три |
| Four | Chetire (cheh•TI•ree) | Четыре |
| Five | Pyaht (PYAHT) | Пять |
| Six | Shest (SHYEHST) | Шесть |
| Seven | Sem (SYEHM) | Семь |
| Eight | Vosem (VAW•syehm) | Восемь |
| Nine | Devat (DYEH•vyeht) | Девять |
| Ten | Desat (DYEH•syeht) | Десять |

## ABOUT RUSSIAN NAMES

In Russia, everyone's first name has three versions. And you can usually tell by a last name if someone is a man or a woman!

| First Name | Nickname | with Patronymic | Last Name |
|---|---|---|---|
| Olga | Olya | Olga Vladimirovna | Surikova |
| Ivan | Vanya | Ivan Vladimirovich | Surikov |
| Vladimir | Volodya | Vladimir Petrovich | Surikov |
| Elena | Lena | Elena Ivanovna | Surikova |
| Yuri | Yura | Yuri Yuryevich | Yuryev |
| Lidiya | Lida | Lidiya Mihaylovna | Pankratova |

Everyone is given a first name. Children are called by their nicknames. Children call adults by their first name plus the patronymic. A patronymic is a person's father's first name plus the masculine or feminine ending. Women use a feminine ending; men use a masculine ending. Girls and women add "a" to their last names. First names are most commonly used in this book to make reading more accessible to English-speaking children.

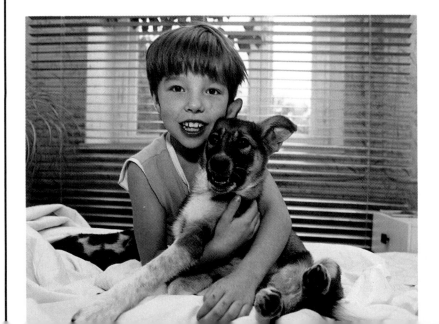

# AFTERWORD

## About Suzdal

Suzdal is one of the oldest towns in Russia. Russian settlers and farmers who were looking for land created homesteads in Suzdal in the tenth century. The first written mention of Suzdal in Russian history books dates back to A.D. 1024, when there was a peasant uprising against the feudal rulers. Over the centuries, Suzdal has survived Mongol attack, Polish invasion, fire, plague, and famine. Modern Suzdal supports itself partly through farming and agriculture and partly through tourism. Some of the buildings in Suzdal date back to the fourteenth century. Today, visitors come from all over Russia and abroad to get a sense of Russian history and architectural development.

## About Russia

Russia is the biggest country in the world. With 6.7 million square miles, Russia is nearly twice as big as the second biggest country, Canada, which has 3.8 million square miles. The People's Republic of China, with 3.7 million square miles, is the third largest. And the United States comes in fourth, with 3.6 million square miles. There are 150 million Russians. More than ten million of them live in Moscow, the world's eleventh biggest city.

Russia has the largest untapped underground oil and gas reserves of any country. Siberia and the Russian Far East contain immense deposits of gold, platinum, aluminum, and uranium. Siberia's Lake Baikal, more than a mile deep and 400 miles long, is the biggest freshwater lake on Earth.

Legend says that Russia was founded in A.D. 862 in Novgorod. In Russian, *novgorod* means "new city." Christianity came to Russia in the tenth century.

Ivan IV (Ivan the Terrible) was the first tsar and is considered to be the founder of the Russian state. Under a succession of rulers such as Peter the Great (1689–1725), Catherine the Great (1762–1796), Alexander II (1855–1881), and Nicholas II (1894–1917), Russia grew in size, expanding into Poland, the Crimea, and central Asia and to the Pacific Ocean.

On October 25, 1917 (now commemorated on November 7), the government was overthrown by the Bolsheviks, led by Vladimir Ilyich Ulyanov, also known as Lenin, and Leon Trotsky. A new government, formed by the Communist party, was installed with Lenin as premier.

The Union of Soviet Socialist Republics, also called the Soviet Union, was established on December 30, 1922. It consisted of Russia and fourteen other republics, including Armenia, Azerbaijan, Belarus, Estonia, Georgia, Kazakhstan, Kyrgyzstan, Latvia, Lithuania, Moldova, Tajikistan, Turkmenistan, Ukraine, and Uzbekistan. After Lenin's death on January 21, 1924, power was seized by Joseph Stalin, who held it until he died on March 6, 1953.

A new series of Communist leaders emerged after Malenkov, who took power the day after Stalin died: Khrushchev, Brezhnev, Andropov, Chernenko, and, finally, Mikhail Gorbachev. Under Gorbachev, the Soviet Union began its shift away from communism and toward democracy.

In August 1991, after an attempted coup against Gorbachev by Communist party loyalists, the new Russian Parliament voted to dissolve the Soviet Union and to disband the Communist party. The Commonwealth of Independent States is an economic union that was formed in December 1991 in which each state or republic has its own government. It consists of Russia and ten of the original Soviet republics. Boris Yeltsin was elected the first president of Russia in 1991.

## About Russians

"Our life is very hard here...."

That is what a grizzled old man in a worn coat told me one cold autumn evening outside a small Suzdal market. He had been quietly watching me as I made photographs in and around the market. A hard wind blew a light snow around us. Finally, he walked over, peered at me, jabbed his finger into the air, then said those words. "Our life is very hard here...." He nodded twice, then walked away into the fading light.

Generations of dictatorship, totalitarianism, and Communist rule taught Russians to be suspicious of strangers, especially strangers who ask a lot of questions and take a lot of pictures. Everyone may have known the truth, but no one dared to speak it. The KGB, responsible for state security, had listeners everywhere. Dissention was not tolerated — dissenters had a way of disappearing all of a sudden. Or at least that is how it was. Today people are changing. They are no longer as fearful as they once were.

After decades of government price controls, Russians became free to experiment with the free-market system and capitalism. The first experiments were disastrous. Shop managers, who for years had been told by the government how much to sell sausage for — say, two rubles for a kilogram (a little more than two pounds) — now had no such limits. Overnight, the price of sausage skyrocketed to 200 rubles for a kilogram, a 100-fold increase. The shop managers were free to set these prices. But the people, whose wages did not increase, could not afford them. Sausages rotted in the stores, unbought, and finally were thrown away. Later shipments of sausages were priced lower, until people started buying them again. And not just sausage prices, but the prices of all kinds of sellable goods rose, then fell. But prices were still ten or twenty or more times what they had been.

Along with capitalism came inflation. Shortly after the first wave of price increases bottomed out, prices began going up

again. When the Russian economic system was opened to foreign currency, the resulting flood of American dollars, German marks, and English pounds further devalued the Russian ruble. Before the economic reforms, American visitors to Russia found the dollar and the ruble worth about the same. That is, you could buy about the same amount of bread, for instance, with one dollar in the United States as you could with one ruble in Russia. But after the reforms, the ruble began to plummet. One dollar became worth 50 rubles, then 100. In late 1992, the dollar was worth 400 rubles. In early 1993, the dollar was worth 700 to 800 rubles. Just buying food became too difficult for some families. Family gardens, which had always been important, became necessary for survival. (Country towns, like Suzdal, with rich, cultivatable soil, have a distinct advantage over big cities like Moscow, where there are almost no places to plant gardens.) Black marketeers began to sell stolen food from the backs of trucks for half of what the stores charged.

Modern Russian families, like the Surikovs, have learned to adapt to these difficult conditions as best as they can. Vladimir paints and repairs automobiles when he is not building and selling furniture. Elena works in a local tourist hotel several days a week to earn extra food money. The children do not get new clothes very often. Meat becomes a luxury. Nothing in the stores, some say, but enough on the tables.

People have become disenchanted with the new reforms. Some have begun to call for a return to the old ways of Communist rule. At least then we had food, they say. They seem to have forgotten the oppression and the people who were taken from their beds in the middle of the night by anonymous policemen, never to be seen again.

Capitalism, democracy, economic reforms, the new Russian government: These all stand on very shaky legs. No one knows whether democracy and capitalism will survive in Russia, or whether they will fail and be replaced by a new breed of communism.

The Russian people are used to hardship and change. But they are not the government. They are strong of spirit and warm of heart. And once you make friends with a Russian, you will not find a better, more committed, friend anywhere.

## Acknowledgments

My deepest thanks to all who helped with this book:

Especially, to the Surikovs — Olga, Ivan, Lena, and Vladimir — for their kindness, patience, and openness.

To Lyubov Ivanovna and Ivan Fyedorovich Balyigin, Lena's parents, and to Nina Alexandrovna Surikova, Vladimir's mother.

To my interpreter, assistant, and best friend in Russia, Mila Yurastova, and her husband, Vladimir, my backgammon partner. And very special thanks to Anna Yakunina, Mila's mother, for her amazing capacity to solve problems and open doors.

To Irina Zaharushkina, for helping me to photograph in the hospital. To Andrey Vasilevich, head surgeon. To Nataliya Boltushkina, the head maternity doctor.

To Oleg Petrov, the mayor of Suzdal, for all of his behind-the-scenes help. To Lieutenant Colonel Valeriy Semenov, chief of police. To Nickolai Kraynov, police officer.

To Yuri Yuryevich Yuryev, master bellringer. To Lidiya Pankratova, Olga's teacher.

To Bishop Valentin, for letting me photograph inside many beautiful churches.

To Sophia Timopheva, president of INTELLECTOUR of Russia, for her invaluable assistance in helping me find the right Russian family.

To Vladimir Masenkov, of Aeroflot, for helping me cut through Aeroflot's red tape.

To all the fine and good people of Suzdal.

Very importantly, to Cynthia Dickstein and OASES, Inc. (formerly the Organization for American-Soviet ExchangeS). Without her help contacting the right people in Russia, this book might never have happened. (Those interested in traveling or working in Russia can reach her at: 324D Harvard St., Cambridge, MA 12139; [617] 864-7717.)

To my editor, Dianne Hess, for her confidence and her masterful editorial direction. To Tracy Mack, for her brilliant editorial assistance. To Marijka Kostiw, for her superb art direction and layout skills.

To Heidi Bradner, for the generous use of her apartment in Moscow.

To Mark Sullivan, news director of the *Cape Cod Times*, for pointing me in the right direction early on.

To Brian Belcher and the staff of Photo Express Image Center, Anchorage, for their exceptional technical support, film processing, and slide duplication.

To Mark Dolan, Paul Souders, Evan R. Steinhauser, and Doug Van Reeth, for their help in editing thousands of photos.

To Ksana Blank, Columbia University, Department of Russian Literature, for fact checking the manuscript.

And to Thérèse, for all else.

> This book was created during a time of monumental change in Russia. While change continues at a rapid pace, this book captures some of the historic moments of *perestroika*.

## About the Photos

The photos in this book were made with Nikon F4 and FM2 cameras, used with 20mm, 55mm micro, 85mm, 180mm, and 300mm lenses. Some of the photos were lit using Norman 400B battery-powered lights triggered with Quantum radio remotes. I also occasionally used a tiny Olympus XA camera when subtlety was important. All photos were shot on Fujichrome film, either ASA 50 or 100.

*This book is dedicated to*
*Tony Dillon, Michael Dinneen, Mark Dolan,*
*Al Grillo, Rob Layman, David Poller, Evan R. Steinhauser,*
*and Doug Van Reeth, the last and the best*
*photo staff of the* Anchorage Times.

*Library of Congress Cataloging-in-Publication Data*
Kendall, Russ.
Russian girl / written and photographed by Russ Kendall.
p.    cm.
Summary: Text and photographs describe the life of a nine-year-old girl and her family in the small Russian town of Suzdal.

ISBN 0-590-45789-6

1. Suzdal (Russia) — Social life and customs — Juvenile literature.
[1. Russia (Federation) — Social life and customs.] I. Title.
DK651.S84K46  1994
947'.77 — dc20      93-13198
CIP
AC

12 11 10 9 8 7 6 5 4 3 2 1      4 5 6 7 8/9

Printed in the U.S.A.          36

First Scholastic printing, March 1994

Designed by Marijka Kostiw